Crush The Competition

How to Go From Overlooked to Overbooked, Create a Brand

Dripping With Your Personality and a Tribe of Raving Fans

TIMEESHA DUNCAN

Chasing Dash Publishing | Atlanta, GA

To book Timeesha Duncan for speaking engagements, visit www.TimeeshaDuncan.com

contents

To My Hubby, Damian aka Biggs – you are my rock. I couldn't thank God for a better partner. You truly complete me. To my family, Jaden, Jordan, Debbie aka Beth, Britnei and Keith aka Boppu and Uncle Ki-ki, Brandon aka Bubba, my Mom and Dad (aka Lu and Gene) and all my amazing friends that support me and hold me down, I love you.

This book is for all my ladies out there that are born hustlers and know there is more to life than working a 9 – 5, getting a paycheck and dying. For all my ladies who go to sleep at night wanting more, dreaming of more and wake up every-day to share their gift with the world. Entrepreneurship is not easy and can sometimes feel extremely lonely and can be a real confidence crusher. It will take you on an emotional roller coaster of excitement, disappointment, happiness, sadness, feelings of being on top of the world and in 2 minutes feel-ing like hiding under a rock never to be seen again. Yep. I know all those feelings because I have had every single one of them, several times over.

That's why this book is for you.

We as women are already taught as young girls to compete, we have to be prettier, thinner, smarter, work harder, be sexi-er, cook better, than the next person.

The truth is, I don't really believe in competition. Well not anymore. I am tired of competing with everyone else. Com-petition doesn't really exist. But most of us don't know that yet. This book is designed to teach you how to eliminate your competition forever. After reading this book you'll learn how to make your competition irrelevant by using what you already have and know to get what you want.

So find a quiet peaceful place, maybe it's your bed, or the park, or your favorite spot on your comfy couch, grab your fa-vorite drink, I prefer a nice glass of wine myself and get ready to have your mind blown!

Xo,

Timeesha

chapter
one

THE SECRET TO DOMINATING
YOUR INDUSTRY AND MAKING
YOUR COMPETITION IRRELEVANT
forever!

So many entrepreneurs are plagued with that ugly green monster – business jealously.

You know what it is – that feeling you get when one of your competitors creates something amazing that you wish you created first?

Or maybe they have 50,000 followers on Facebook and Instagram and you barely have 500. And it seems like their audience craves anything and everything they release into the atmosphere.

Yeah...that feeling.

We've all had it at least once in our life.

But I got the anecdote to make that feeling go away once and for all.

So without further ado, here is my first jewel dropping knowledge tip:

Forget what everybody else is doing.

We are human and nosy by nature, and with a click of a button on our electronic devices, we can secretly peek into the private world of anyone without being detected. It's addictive I know, but it needs to stop today.

You don't need to "follow" people to stay in the know with the latest trends. Following certain people only takes away your creativity and lowers your chances of creating anything original. It's ok to follow people in your industry, but if you are following anyone that makes you feel inferior, or if you've ever said to yourself, "I could never do that," (even if you thought it in your head it still counts), you need to unfollow them. Your social media platforms should inspire and encourage you, not make you question or second guess your own abilities. This applies to friends as well. You have to be honest with yourself and protect your heart, mind and soul. It's not personal.

Do whatever you gotta do to get them off your radar, unfollow them on Instagram, Twitter, Facebook, Pinterest, Periscope unsubscribe from their mailing list...

Do it, and do it now. I'll wait...

(Cue in Jeopardy hold music)

Done? Ok. Good Girl.

Don't you just feel like an annoying monkey was taken off your back?

You can never be successful worrying about someone else's success. Learn how to Mind Your Business and then you will watch it Grow.

The only person you should try to be better than is the person you were yesterday.

Believe it or not, now you've just freed up a bunch of time to focus on what's really important – creating your irresistible offer and crushing the competition with your pointy toe 4 1/2 inch leopard print stilettos.

News Flash:
The best way to stand out in a
crowded market is to be uniquely you.

I know you're thinking... "Ok, Timeesha, what the heck does that really mean?"

But before I explain what I mean by that, I have to clear something up first...

As entrepreneurs we always think that in order to stand out we have to be this over the top extroverted personality and have charisma the size of Madison Square Garden.

But let me tell you honey child, I am none of those things and I will never be.

You don't need to be an extrovert, or have the personality of Oprah Winfrey.

You do need to have charisma, but it's the stuff we're made of that make us who we are. There is no rulebook on the type of person you have to be.

You can be the nice, girl by day - Diva by night Bombshell like Beyoncé.

You can be the sexy, sultry, bad girl like Rihanna.

You can be a no nonsense, sophisticated, problem solver who wears white coats and drinks vintage wine like Olivia Pope.

You can be the loud mouth, trash talker that everybody loves like Cookie Lyons.

You can be the change the world, motherly type like Michelle Obama.

Charisma is defined as: a special personal quality or power of an individual making her capable of influencing or inspiring large numbers of people.

So Your Charisma is whatever the stuff YOU are made of.

There is no one specific type of Charisma you need to possess.

There is NO ONE LIKE YOU IN THE WORLD.

NOPE. Not even your twin sister.

Why not take advantage of this benefit instead of trying to be a second rate version of someone else's original?

Someone who is multi-dimensional is more appealing and will get their true fans pumping up their fists like a bunch of teens at the Jersey Shore more than someone who is trying to blend in like everybody else.

Ok so back to your question... "Ok, Timeesha, what the heck does that really mean?".

Well darling, it means that you need to showcase your passions and your pleasures into your business.

This combination is a scrumptious recipe for instant girl crush love and will give you the edge over your competition, which equals more Cash Money for you... More Moola Bae Bae, (in my Lil' Wayne voice)

Here's another news flash for you:

When you sell your services and products, you are not really selling your service at all... you are selling a relationship.

Your expertise in a particular subject matter, (for example, wedding planning) cannot realistically be measured.

It's the perception your dream client has of you, that inspires her to buy from you. She has to feel connected to who you are, and what you stand for.

I know you're thinking... But what if I lose clients?

It's an understandable concern, but it's rooted out of FEAR.

(That's the nastiest four-letter word I know for business pros).

But do you really wanna work with someone who makes you feel afraid to say you secretly love The Kardashians and Real Housewives of Atlanta and will think you are a total idiot because you do?

Um. Absolutely not!

You wouldn't want to work with someone who despises who you really are, right?

Think about all that time and energy you would have spent playing the role of someone else every time you were around them.

That gives me a migraine just thinking about it.

You deserve to work with someone that not only allows you to be yourself, but appreciates the fact that you love the Kardashians and Real Housewives and can spend hours gossiping with you about that last episode of Empire.

When you start weaning those people out of your life, things will flow much easier and effortlessly.

In the next chapter we are going to give you a little makeover and show you exactly how to do this.

chapter
two

HOW TO TELL YOUR UNIQUE
STORY TO SOUND JUICIER THAN
A GEORGIA PEACH IN THE
summertime!

The easiest and most effective way to stand out in any market and make your competition irrelevant is to tell YOUR unique story.

Everyone has one...Basically, why do you do what you do? What motivated you to start your business?

People want to know who the woman (or man) is behind the brand. It makes your business multi-dimensional, it gives it depth and takes on a persona and develops a personality all its on.

Don't you agree that you feel more connected to brands when you know the back story of how they got started, or what their purpose or mission is in helping their ideal clients?

Your story doesn't mean you have to come from nothing and be piss poor and then overnight you created an amazing product that made you a millionaire. Those stories are great novellas but the reality is most of us don't have that type of story. Maybe your story is not that dramatic. It doesn't have to be a tear jerker.

It could just be that you were tired of not being able to find a bra that fit you because of your breast size and you decided you wanted to create custom bras for women who are top heavy and still want to feel sexy and not have to wear a bra that looks like its for their 80 year old Granny.

As a matter of fact, do you know who Sara Blakely is? She is the woman who created Spanx. She was tired of not having something to wear under her clothes that didn't show a panty line (and all the wrinkles and dimples) so she created Spanx. Simple. And now she is a billionaire.

So really sit down and think about why you do what you do. And choose what you really want to share and be sincere.

Why do you do what you do? (AKA what is your why?)

_____

_____

_____

_____

_____

_____

What is your mission? (What do you want to accomplish?)

_____

_____

_____

_____

_____

What is your vision? (Where do you see your business going long term?)

_____

_____

_____

_____

_____

How did you get started?

_____

_____

_____

_____

_____

_____

Did you have any unique turning points in your life that motivated you to start your own business, did you lose your job, have an accident, had a child, what was it that made you decide to go after your dream?

_____

_____

_____

_____

_____

What are some ways you can start a different or new trend in your industry?

_____

_____

_____

_____

_____

_____

Brainstorm a few here:

_____

_____

_____

_____

_____

_____

_____

_____

_____

What can you do differently that your competitors are doing (or not doing)?

_____

_____

_____

_____

_____

Create a tab or page on your website and even on your Facebook Page if possible and call it "My Story" or "About Me" or "Why I Started…"

I created my business because when I started my wedding planning business, their wasn't any specific information to teach me how to brand and get clients, only topics on how to become a wedding planner – but I needed to know how to run a business and so when I found how and became an expert at it, I wanted to share with other female entrepreneurs who were struggling with the same thing.

The main reason I created the Quit Your 9-5 Academy is because I know how difficult it is to juggle having a full-time job and run a business. And I was a mom with two kids and had a husband who had been laid off – so I felt I had to stay in my job, but I was suffering. So once I figured out how to create the perfect exit plan from my job and create a successful biz, I wanted to show other people who were suffering like me how to do the same thing.

Nobody died. I didn't have to live in my car, although I did have to file bankruptcy and lost everything I had, but you can read about that in my next book. ☺

So be authentic and true to you and your why and who cares what everyone else thinks!

chapter
three

HOW TO INFUSE YOUR
PERSONALITY INTO YOUR BRAND
AND CREATE INSTANT GIRL
CRUSH *love!*

When you start to showcase who you really are into your brand, you will turn off some people.

You will even feel vulnerable and a bit silly at first. But you will be building the ultimate fan base that is completely addicted to you and inspired by you and your business.

So It's time to let that little personality of yours come on out!

So first let's talk about your passions: These are the things you love to do all the time that you would do for free, you never get tired of doing this and you feel you are the best version of yourself when you are doing it.

For example: I'm extremely passionate about Dancing.

I have been dancing all my life.

I absolutely love everything about dance.

I could watch So You Think You Can Dance all day (in fact, one of my former students, Zack Everhart, was a finalist in season 11 by the way...)

I could perform every day of my life and never get bored or tired.

I love choreographing new dance routines.

I love teaching dance.

I love producing dance shows.

I would dance for $10,000.

I would dance for $0.10.

I have danced with celebrities like Jennifer Lopez.

I have danced at Karaoke bars.

I will never get tired of dancing.

Put music on right now...I'm probably dancing.

That is an example of a <u>true</u> passion.

Now here is an example of something I thought was a passion...

I love graphic design.

I am obsessed with pretty papers, art and creating new things.

I decided to take a class in Photoshop and quickly realized, I'm not passionate about this at all.

Learning all the tools and techy stuff started to give me a headache.

I felt so much better hiring someone else to create what was in my head rather than do it myself.

That wasn't a real passion.

Your passions should make you feel whole, more alive. It's something you love to do that you will most likely ALWAYS do or practice throughout your life.

Ok. Your turn....

I want you to write down 10 things you are passionate about at this very moment. (Not things that you loved doing when you were 10 and haven't done in years).

1 _____

2 _____

3 _____

4 _____

5 _____

6 _____

7 _____

8 _____

9 _____

10 _____

Now let's talk about guilty pleasures.

These are the things that make you tingle inside, but are not activities you would want to do all day, every day, in fact, too much of it would probably make you sick.

My guilty pleasures: Reality TV.

I love watching a good cat-fighting episode of Real Housewives, but I don't tune in every week when it comes on, I'm probably catching a rerun or Sunday marathon of the show. Too much of it can be annoying, but I love a good scandal and gossip so I watch it (with a glass of wine or chocolate ice-cream...my other guilty pleasures.)

Got it?

Ok. Your turn.... I want you to write down 10 juicy guilty pleasures you have:

1 _____

2 _____

3 _____

4 _____

5 _____

6 _____

7 _____

8 _____

9 _____

10 _____

The key is to try to get them all down on paper and then focus on the top 1-3 main passions + guilty pleasures you have that your audience will appreciate and love you for.

Top 3 Passions

1

2

3

Top 3 Guilty Pleasures

1

2

3

Now here is the fun part.

What passions do you have that are similar to the ones your dream clients have?

_____

_____

_____

_____

_____

_____

What guilty pleasures do you have that are similar to the ones your dream clients have?

_____

_____

_____

_____

_____

_____

If you can't think of any that you have in common, think of it this way...

What passions do you want to be known for?

_____

_____

_____

_____

_____

What guilty pleasures do you want to be known for?

_____

_____

_____

_____

_____

_____

Don't be afraid to show people what makes you uniquely you.

Ok all of this sounds good Timeesha but where exactly do I put this stuff?

I thought you'd never ask... Your About Page on your website is a perfect place to start!

Did you know your about page is the hottest place on your website that gets the most action? Statistics show that the about page of any website gets the most views.

Yep.

That's right honey.

People want to know about you.

This is the perfect opportunity to give em' a little taste of why you are the Rockstar (insert title here) for them.

Now, hold the phone for a minute... Your about page should be 90% about how you can help them with their struggles and/or desires and 10% about you.

But you can certainly open your about page with a mini bio of who you are.

For example, mine is:

I'm Timeesha and I work with women who want to take their business from basic to bombshell status.

I teach them how to get their dream clients addicted to them like Beyoncé's Beyhive and Crush the Competition all while making it feel like a spa day with your BFF.

When I'm not helping women create their new bombshell life, I'm choreographing dance routines for theater productions, trying out new fancy restaurants with my hubby, being an Avenger in our Superhero cave with my sons (I'm always Thor for some reason), or craving over the latest fashion trends in Vogue Magazine.

Doesn't that make me sound like a fun well rounded person you would want to get to know and work with?

Every bit of that statement is 100% true, even the Thor part. Feel free to follow the same script with your own tantalizing passions and guilty pleasures!

I'M *(INSERT NAME)* AND I WORK WITH *(INSERT IDEAL CLIENTS)* WHO WANT/NEED/HATE *(INSERT WHAT THEY WANT OR WHAT THEY DON'T WANT)* WHILE MAKING IT FEEL LIKE *(ULTIMATE PLEASURE!)*

WHEN I'M NOT HELPING/TEACHING/SHOWING *(INSERT WHAT YOU DO FOR YOUR CLIENTS)* I'M *(INSERT 1-2 PASSIONS)* AND *(1-2 GUILTY PLEASURES HERE)*.

Here's another example:

I'm Tiffany Simone and I work with millennial moms who want to lose those last ten unruly pounds of baby fat after pregnancy, all while making it feel like a day at the beach.

When I'm not helping my clients get their sexy back, I'm somewhere watching a horror flick, writing poems or visiting new local eateries.

YOUR CONTENT

You can also take the opportunity to use the new and improved you in your newsletters, blog posts, eBooks and the list goes on and on.

This is a perfect opportunity to share your expertise on a particular subject that you know your dream clients would appreciate.

For example, since I'm the queen of dance, when I was practicing wedding planning, I could write an article on "The Top Show-Stopping Wedding Dances of 2016"

Or if you're a caterer who loves to travel, you could blog about "My Favorite Resort Picks for Honeymoon Eats."

Or if you are a photographer who loves makeup, you can write an article about "Getting Red Carpet Ready for Your Wedding Day."

Got it? Now it's your turn to try it here:

What are some blog titles/ videos/ tutorials/classes/newsletters you could write about that showcase your passions + guilty pleasures and professional expertise:

_____

_____

_____

_____

_____

_____

_____

_____

_____

_____

_____

_____

_____

_____

_____

_____

_____

_____

_____

_____

_____

_____

_____

_____

YOUR FREE OFFER:

Think about your free offer you provide to your dream client... (If you don't know what I'm talking about, you gotta get my Addicted book where I dish the tea on how to make one that's totally irresistible!)

What would your dream client appreciate from you for free that you could offer to get her on your mailing list?

Is it an e-book on the top 10 money-saving tips for couponing?

Is it a guide on the Top 5 Celebrity Wedding Hacks?

Is it a list of things they need to know before they hire their next photographer?

Be that go to source for all things (insert your industry here) in your industry.

Once you start to infuse your personality into your offerings and create your own runway, you will start to build your very own unique tribe that will swarm to you like bees to honey and anticipate your offer.

Your competition will evaporate into thin air and you will reign supreme as the go-to-girl in your industry.

chapter four

HOW TO WRITE JUICY + COMPELLING CONTENT THAT'S HOTTER THAN AN EPISODE OF YOUR FAVORITE PRIMETIME *show!*

The key to writing juicy sales copy that motivates your clients to buy is to talk to them as you would talk to your BFF.

When someone reads your writing, you want them to feel as if you are talking directly to them, as if you were standing right in front of them, calling them by name.

You want them to be able to feel an instant connection with you, even though they probably don't even know you.

People get all anxious and sweaty when they have to think about writing content for their website or blog, but it's a really simple process.

When you get ready to write down something, I want you to think as if you were talking to your BFF. What would you say to her (or him)?

Would you say, "Hello friend, I have recently designed a dress that will assist you in accomplishing your needs to lose inches off your waist and gain confidence in yourself.

OR

Would you say:

I made the perfect little black dress that makes you feel sexy, slim and chic!

Remember, intimacy is key baby. You want to add a personal touch to your writing.

Try to stay away from words like "us" and "we" if you are the only one rocking it in your biz.

It makes you sound stuffy and less personal. Remember, you want people to be attracted to you and want to work with you and only you.

You still want to sound professional when you speak to your clients whether it be live or written word, but don't be afraid to let your hair down and speak as you would to someone you really like and feel comfortable with. The more personal and relaxed you are with your ideal clients, the more they will feel connected to you.

"YOU" VS. "I"

When you're writing your content for your sales page, use the word "you" more than you use the word "I".

For example, if you were looking to hire a photographer for your event, which one would you want to hire:

Photographer A:

I have been working as a photographer for 15 years and only work with the highest quality cameras. I use a CANON RTF-6530098HQP to capture bright, eye-catching images. I will work with you for 8 hours and I will bring my 2nd camera-man so we can make sure we capture all the elements of your event.

Photographer B:

Your wedding day is the most important moment of your new life. I don't focus on time, but focus on making sure you can re-live your most special moments, like the moment your hus-band glances at you for the first time as you walk down the aisle, or the tear your dad sheds as he gives his little girl away. I always bring a second shooter with me so we can make sure we capture all elements of your event.

They pretty much said the same thing, but doesn't photographer B make you want to take out your checkbook right now?

That's because he painted a picture of the benefits YOU receive from hiring him, not talking about all his fancy shmancy skills and devices.

Sell the benefits – talk more about what they get by using the word YOU. When you do this, they instantly feel like you are talking directly to them , and helps them see themselves with exactly what they want from you.

USE THEIR LANGUAGE

What words does she say to describe how she feels, what words does she say to describe her problem?

Once they tell you what their problem is – regurgitate this back into your business using their language.

What word or phrases does your dream client use to describe her problem?

_____

_____

_____

What are common phrases your dream clients say?

_____

_____

_____

Use those same words in your marketing (website, sales page, emails, advertising campaigns) because that's the language that will resonate with her.

For example, when I send out emails to my subscribers list, I get a ton of emails back from people thanking me for my email, and I get a lot of comments, like, *"OMG you read my mind! "*, *"This hit home for me"*... or *"that was just what I needed to hear today"*... and that's because I listen to what my clients say, I have empathy for them so I'm compassionate to their feelings.

This is why its so important to know your dream clients inside and out so you can speak her language and know what she's thinking before she thinks it. It's not hard to do, you just have to take the time to interview people who fit the bill of being your dream clients!

Got an email list already? Send them a survey and ask them these two important questions:

1. What are they struggling with right now?
2. What do they want instead?

You can ask more questions if you want, but those two questions are enough to get client magnetic language to use!

If you don't have an email list its ok. Just seek out a few friends, colleagues or a random person off the street who fits the bill of what your ideal client would be like and ask them the same questions.

Don't pass go without doing this step. It works!

TAKE A TIP FROM
YOUR FAVORITE MAGAZINE!

Magazines have always been one of my guilty pleasures. I get all tingly inside when I see a Glamour or Elle Décor in the mailbox! I cant wait to tear it open with a bowl of Chocolate ice-cream and Caramel Cake and get the inside scoop to how celebs look flawless and get new trend ideas!

You know that feeling you get when your favorite glossy hits newsstands? That's exactly the way you want your dream clients to feel when you post a new blog article – they cant wait to get their hands on it!

You know what makes magazines so popular and irresistible? They focus on the problems and desires we have!

If you go to any newsstand in your local grocery store right now, I'll bet you'll see at least 3 magazines that have some new craze diet on it... "How to Lose 5lbs in 5 minutes!"... you know why? Because women are constantly struggling with their weight and want a lose weight fast anecdote.

This is exactly why you need to know who your dream clients are and what problems (or desires) they have!

The magazine cover and content in a Redbook Magazine is way different than the cover and content of Lucky Magazine... because their audiences are very different and they know that.

So let's put this to work!

What are your 3 favorite magazines and what do you love about them?

_____

_____

_____

_____

_____

_____

What type of images do you see on the cover of the magazine?

_____

_____

_____

_____

_____

What headline(s) caught your immediate attention?

_____

_____

_____

_____

_____

_____

Now, here is the fun part!

There is something to learn from reading magazines. You could have written the best blog post or email in the world. You've spent hours, maybe even days creating it and know this post is going to be a game changer for your business. You hit "publish", and sit back and wait for the comments and requests to come in… but then….

Nothing. You hear crickets.

Here is the problem, your content might be amazing, but it's the title that is going to get someone to actually open it up and read it. And if your title is lame, or doesn't speak to your audience's problems or desires, they will ignore it.

There is a quick and easy fix to this though. You can write sizzling, scintillating blog and email titles for your readers too, by taking a page from your favorite magazine!

Write down 10 topics you love from your favorite magazine, exactly how you see it. Then write down how you can remix this title to work for your biz.

SO HERE ARE SOME EXAMPLES:

This title is from Glamour Magazine:

"25 Best Trends for 2015"

Here is a remix title for a Business Coach:

"15 Blazing New Business Trends for 2016"

Here is another example from Lucky Magazine:

"A New Way to Perfect Skin"

Here is a remix for a Wedding Planner:

"A New Way to a Perfect Wedding Day"

Ok, so let's get to work girly:

MAG TITLE:

_____

YOUR REMIXED TITLE:

_____

MAG TITLE:

_____

YOUR REMIXED TITLE:

_____

MAG TITLE:

_____

YOUR REMIXED TITLE:

_____

MAG TITLE:

_____

YOUR REMIXED TITLE:

_____

MAG TITLE:

_____

YOUR REMIXED TITLE:

_____

MAG TITLE:

_____

YOUR REMIXED TITLE:

_____

MAG TITLE:

_____

YOUR REMIXED TITLE:

_____

You will be well on your way to creating juicy titles and sales copy that will knock the socks off your dream clients and keep them wanting more!

chapter
five

HOW TO CREATE A TRIBE OF
RAVING FANS ON SOCIAL
MEDIA THAT CONVERT INTO
sales!

Ok so here's the deal… Social Media is the fastest way to get yourself in front of your ideal clients in droves. With a click of a button (or app) millions of people who never knew you were alive now have access to see your hot biz and what you have to offer.

Thanks to social media I've had the opportunity to work with clients in Sydney, Australia, London, Nigeria and the Caribbean! So yeah, social media is a big deal.

But, let's keep it real.

It can be truly overwhelming to say the least.

But don't fret my beauty. I am going to show you how to rock it on social media by using these simple yet powerful techniques.

However, I have to put this disclaimer out before we start this chapter... I don't care what you've heard. You don't have to be on every single platform. I believe in spending your time on the 2 -3 most popular platforms your ideal clients hang out. For example, if your clients are not on Linkedin, then why are you wasting time on there? And that goes for any other platform.

My tribe hangout predominantly on Instagram, Facebook and now Periscope, so that's where you will find me on at least one or all of these every single day.

Make it a habit to be where your people are and be consistent in your posting. People like to follow brands they can trust and rely on.

Ok, now that I got that out, let's get started with my fave platform… Instagram!

INSTAGRAM

Now here are 10 steps to really rock it on Instagram and build a community that adore and love you and anything you put in the atmosphere:

#1: YOUR INSTAGRAM FEED SHOULD LOOK LIKE A MAGAZINE

Think Pinterest but with conversation

If you truly want to attract new followers to your page, you've got to give them a reason to want to follow you.

You should post with intention to gain new followers who don't know you, not for the people who already follow you.

Remember, when new people come to your page, they are looking at the first 6-12 pictures you post, and if they are all poor quality images, or you taking not so flattering selfies, or pictures of you and your cat, Mr. Pickles, you probably wont get a lot of followers.

You have to remember, what you post also comes up in your followers feed. I'm quick to delete someone who posts stupidity because I don't want to see that everyday.

#2: YOUR OVERALL PAGE NEEDS TO BE THE ESSENCE OF WHAT YOU OFFER AND WANT TO BE KNOWN FOR

It's ok to post personal pictures, in fact I encourage it if you are a business of one, but make sure that 99% of those personal pics still correlate back to your biz.

So for example, if you are a caterer, your page doesn't have to be just the finished product of something you prepared.

You can post about the food you cook, give recipes, or show beautifully plated meals.

If you are a stylist, post collages on different outfits, swoon worthy pumps and accessories, celebrity fashion or ask your followers to choose your next #OOTD. (Outfit of the Day).

A great example of this is one of my besties, Kesha Lambert of Kesha Lambert Photography (@keshalambert).

Kesha is a celebrity photographer, and takes some of the most beautiful wedding photography shots I have ever seen.

Her page is literally a visual portfolio of her work. Below is a screenshot of just some of the goodness she puts into the atmosphere.

And what I like about her page is that she occasionally will post a super cute picture of her family or her boys, but she always does it in a way that correlates to what she does best – take amazing pictures!

#3: SHARE SOME BEHIND THE SCENES STUFF

We have an obsession of seeing what people are doing "Behind the Scenes". So post a little bit about what goes into making your business and YOU so fabulous.

Are you buying supplies for a floral arrangement? Post an image of the prep or the flowers before they are cut and styled into a beautiful arrangement.

#4: MAKE YOUR PAGE PUBLIC

Nobody is going to follow a private page.

Remember, we are not talking about the people who already know and love you, we are talking about people who want to get to know you.

If your page is private, you're automatically sending a message that you are not interested in getting any new friends.

Think of it this way, how would you feel if you went to a store in the middle of the day and it was closed?

You're not going to send a note to the owner and "request" them to open the door... you are going to keep it moving. And that's what people will do when they come to your private page – Keep It Movin'.

If you want to keep things private (like pictures of your kids) consider making a personal page for friends and family that know you, but your business page should always be public.

#5. DON'T BUY FOLLOWERS

So many people get caught up with the idea of looking popular so they go out and buy followers to look important.

But here's the thing…you can have 50,000 followers but if none of them buy your products or services, what's the point?

Now, I am not talking about marketing your page to real targeted followers via Facebook Ads or Instagram Marketing.

I'm talking about just paying for accounts that have no intention of taking any action on your page.

If you take nothing away from this little lesson, then remember this: Your posts should turn into profits.

If they don't, you need to go back to the drawing board. And guess what else? When you buy followers people can tell.

I can't tell you how many pages I've seen where they have 30,000 followers, but only have 10 likes at most on their pictures.

Now... Are you trying to tell me that out of 30,000 followers, only 10 people find interest in what you post?

Very unlikely. And if that doesn't convince you maybe this will... Instagram is cracking down on the fake accounts and deleting them. So you can look like you have 5,000 followers today and tomorrow you have 25.

So be careful.

#6. USE INSTAGRAM'S PHOTO ENHANCER TO BRIGHTEN YOUR PHOTOS

I can bet you that 85% of the beautiful pages you follow that have the most stunning images are not taken with a professional camera. That honestly takes up to much time and work.

They are using photo-editing apps straight from their phone to brighten and enhance their pictures.

You might have a great shot but it might be too dark… use one of these apps to give it a lift and make it pop.

There are tons of photo enhancing apps out there. They even have apps to smooth out your skin! Instagram now has it's own photo enhancing capabilities to brighten your pictures.

Trust me, I don't have time to figure anything out, so these work perfect for me. A beautiful page like Coco Tafoya's @deluxemodern uses Tadaa for her pictures!

Always check your entire feed after you post something. If you post a picture that doesn't compliment your entire feed, delete it and save it for another time.

Sometimes we put things out there because we think it looks good, but it doesn't do anything for the overall brand. Again, save those things for personal (or private) pages and post with your entire visual brand in mind.

@DELUXEMODERN

#7 - DON'T BE AFRAID TO ADVERTISE ON INSTAGRAM

Studies show that people are shopping for things via Instagram, and I'm living proof of that. I get several inquiries a week just from people seeing my posts on Instagram alone.

Instagram is the new way to market your products, services and events online.

So take advantage of this platform and "shout it out"!

Running a special holiday or just because sale? Post it on your page.

Going live on Periscope? Post it on your page.

Have a workshop, webinar or event you want to invite peeps to…post it on your page!

#8: TALK TO YOUR FOLLOWERS!

The same love you want to get from your new community of followers is the same love they need to feel right back.

Showing your followers that you care and actually took the time to show them some love will do wonders for your following.

So when someone comments on your post, reply back to them.

If someone starts following you show them some love, and like a few of their pages, or even follow them back if you like their feed.

Ask questions at the end of your post to get people in the habit of commenting! And one last thing – ask people to share your stuff!

Believe it or not, when you ask for the share or the tag, people will do it.

You can simply add a line at the bottom of your posts that says, "Tag 3 friends who would love this." I have even created a location that says "Tag a Friend" so I can easily add it to a post I think is sharable. Liking and sharing posts leads to new followers (which leads to new followers!)

#9: THE RIGHT WAY TO USE #HASHTAGS

Hashtags are great, and are imperative to bringing unique traffic to your posts. Hashtags are like labels that tell people what your posts are about. But if you use too many hashtags in your post, it makes you look spammy and desperate. So here are a few tricks to using hashtags the right way.

1. Don't use generic hashtags like "instagood" or "business", use targeted ones that are specific to your industry. This makes it easy for your dream clients to find you on Instagram and this way you don't get riffraff followers that don't have an interest in buying your products or services.

2. Put your hashtags in the comments section of your post, instead of the actual post.

Instagram allows you to use up to 30 hashtags for every post. So you want to take advantage of this and use every single keyword (aka hashtag) that will bring your ideal clients to your page.

Now here is something you probably didn't know (so come in closer, this will be our little secret). The only way to make your hashtags searchable is to add them to the comments. Now that Instagram has changed it's algorithm, it determines how it will show your post to your followers based on the engagement your posts get. So you want to make sure you are utilizing your comments section properly!

Always, always, always post, and then add your hashtags as the first comment under your post. This will make them searchable to Instagram and will help you not look spammy or thirsty for followers. Why you ask? Well because after 2 people comment under your first comment, the comment sections gets minimized and you don't see the first 3 anymore! They still work, but they are hidden. So now all you see is your great post (without all the spammy stuff!)

And no you don't have to type 30 hashtags each time (because I know that's what you're thinking) simply pick the best 30 hashtags for your business and type them in a note on your smart phone. Everyone has a notes app. When you post to Instagram just simply copy and paste your hashtags as the first comment under each post and viola!

#10: SAY HELLO!

When you like and comment on other people's pages, they will see you in their timeline and will be more inclined to come check your page out and see who you are.

If you really want to be noticed, like at least 3 pictures and comment on at least 1.

Everybody reads the comments people leave and when you do this consecutively in a row, your name pops up in their feed at least 4 times, so guess what, they are going to check you out to see who this person is who's liking their stuff.

But don't overdo it, because then you will look like a stalker!

The 3 to 1 rule is a good one to stick to! But remember, You have to follow rule #1 in order for this to work effectively. If your feed is filled with beautiful images, 9 times of out 10 – you will gain a new follower. If your feed is filled with junk... then it probably won't work for you.

What I love most about this tip is that you have gained a real follower that will like and comment on your posts and maybe even buy your products. Way more valuable than a bunch of fake followers.

LIVE STREAM

I know, I know. It can be daunting to say the least. But video and specifically live streaming is doing wonders for entrepreneurs! Live streaming gives you the ability to get in front of your ideal clients and allows them to see you...the real you. People love to connect with real live people. Live streaming platforms like Periscope and Facebook Live (and whatever else might jump on the seen before I'm done writing this line) has allowed people to instantly connect with fans from all over the world in a matter of seconds.

While it can be intimidating, here is why you need to be using this platform for your business: It allows you to make a real connection with your fans – think mini infomercial in a short period of time.

You talk, we watch, we buy.

You can make a connection with someone within a relatively short period of time, and they can decide whether or not they like you and want to buy your products or services in a matter of minutes, instead of seeding them for months with email marketing and so on.

If you're shy don't worry – introverts are making a killing on these platforms!!

Now, when you go on these platforms here are a few quick tips to make your broadcasts successful:

1. Introduce yourself and what you do every time (always assume you have new followers watching that don't know you). This tells them why they need to continue watching.

2. Tell them what they can expect - "Today I am showing you 3 ways to grow your hair."

3. Get to the point. People will lose interest quickly, so introduce yourself, tell them what they are going to learn and then get to the teaching!

4. Engage with your viewers. Don't spend the whole time doing this but welcome your peeps and thank them for watching you.

5. Always have a Call To Action. What do you want them to do? Buy your book? Follow you on Instagram, download your free ebook, share this video with their friends? Always ask for what you want.

FACEBOOK

Facebook is unique because you can advertise your business to targeted ideal clients that are already known for wanting, liking and buying your type of services.

Create a Business Page that is separate from your personal page and create a Facebook Like ad to bring traffic to your site.

Facebook Ads are all about the images, so create an eye-catching image that personifies what your business is about. And say things like "Like this ad for tips on how to lose 10lbs in 30 days."

HERE IS AN EXAMPLE OF A FACEBOOK AD I USED:

 Bombshell Business Academy

Join me on this live free workshop where you will learn:

1. The inside secret to crushing your competition and making them irrelevant forever!

2. Branding secrets from some of the most popular multi-million dollar brands in the industry today!

3. How to brand a tribe of raving fans that love you and buy anything you sell like Beyonce's Beyhive!

4. A simple (but neglected trick to start getting instant girl crush love to stand out from your competition immediately.

Free Live Workshop - How to Stand Out From Your Competition and Make Them Irrelevant Forever!

Create a Facebook Group that is specifically for members that join your email list, or social media platforms and within the private group you can show them some special love by answering questions they may have, which will show you as the expert!

Contribute to other Facebook groups that are related to your business by giving advice, tips or tricks that the members can use which will make them want to go and check you out! Don't sell because no one likes people like that, but occasionally give value.

I started my branding business by joining Facebook groups where flocks of my ideal clients hung out, and contributed to the discussions. And that's how I got my first few clients!

You can also get valuable feedback to use for your own business in finding out what your ideal clients are struggling with and want and need and then create something in your business as the answer.

chapter
six

HOW TO GET

FEATURED IN BLOGS AND

magazines!

A surefire way to stand out from your competition and get instant credibility (and girl crush love) is to have you and/or your biz featured in the press.

The perception is, if you are featured in the press than your biz must be awesome! If they are paying attention it, then I must pay attention to it too!

People want to see that other people are interested in what you have to say, and if one of those people just happens to be a reputable magazine, blog or even TV Show, then that's gold for your business!

So here's what you have to do:

First, start creating your wish list!

Find the blogs, magazines and or TV shows that you think would be interested in your biz.

An easy way to knock this out without feeling like a full on snooze fest, is to go to your fave bookstore with a nice tall Caramel Macchiato (or whatever your favorite drink from Starbucks is) and sift through the magazine section.

Every magazine in just about every genre is there. And you can look through the glossies to see who the editor is. (without having to buy all of them!)

You can do the same thing on blogs – every blog has a contact us or even a Media or Advertise page.

Another great {sneaky} tip – check out who your competitors have been featured by. Chances are if they have gotten a feature with X company, that same company might be interested in featuring you too.

Dream big, but be realistic. Don't just shoot for the big name, high-profile peeps if you're just starting out as they tend to look for more seasoned people that have a buzz around them. Local peeps or not so big name people that are on the "come-up" are not bad to explore either! Don't discount the little guys. One feature will lead to many more.

Then get to looking for their contact information.

Every reputable magazine has a website. So go to their website and see who the editor is, or search for the Media/ Advertise / Contact Us page, and they will tell you exactly who to contact to get featured.

Another great tip especially if you want to be featured on a blog – is to contribute!

Be a source of information for them. Comment on their blog posts, and comment on their social media posts too. Show that you care. Don't think they don't read your comments – they do! Trust me. They need feedback from their readers to create their own content, so trust me they are paying attention to you!

And make sure you know what their business or blog is about before you try to pitch them on featuring you. The worst thing you can do is provide content that is not relevant to what they do.

It shows that you really didn't take the time to research them, you just want a feature for personal gain and that's a no go with anyone.

When you reach out to these outlets, don't just talk about yourself and why you are a good fit to be featured in their magazine. They are in the business to get people to read their magazine – so you want to talk about why your business/idea/service/product is great for... THEIR READERS.

Here is an example of a good pitch:

Dear xx,

My name is Olivia Smith and I'm the founder of Love My Curves, a program for women who are struggling with self-esteem issues due to their weight. I know your audience struggles with building their self-confidence and would love to share 10 confidence builders that would help them love themselves more, especially for women who are struggle with confidence due to their weight. Would you be interested in a story idea on the "10 Ways to Start Loving Your Curves?"

This way, its not about you or them – it's about their readers. And if they feel their readers will love your story – you're in!

chapter
seven

HOW TO CREATE STRATEGIC
PARTNERS TO HELP BUILD YOUR
brand!

If you want to be connected in the industry, you have to give value.

There might be someone you are dying to work with, or to know and even get them to lay just one eyeball on your business.

Well, how can you contribute to what they are already doing?

The best way to get them to notice you... is to give them value.

So what does that mean?

Well, if you like something they did, send them an email!

No matter how "big" or "small" you think someone is in the industry, everyone loves to hear positive feedback on how they have either helped you, or inspired you.

Make it a habit to send one email out a day to tell someone you haven't worked with but would like to, how they inspired, motivated or empowered you. Is it someone on Instagram or Periscope that you recently fell in love with and want to be on their radar?

Send them an email. Keep it short and sweet and give value, don't ask for anything in exchange.

Start your list!

Name 10 people that you can email to show them some girl crush love:

_____

_____

_____

_____

_____

_____

_____

_____

Is it a competitor in your local market that you would like to partner with? List 3 businesses here:

1 _____

2 _____

3 _____

Start the conversation by saying hello and thanking them for what they did for you. Don't ask for anything (yet)!

Send someone a handwritten card!

Everyone loves to get stuff in the mail. Nothing says personal then a handwritten card or note they receive in the mail.

If you've met someone at a networking event and want to maintain the relationship, send them a note saying how much you enjoyed meeting them.

Make sure to ask people how YOU can help THEM. (Not the other way around). You never want to appear as a taker, you want to appear as someone who can be of value to the person you want to work with.

This is especially true if they don't know you. The only thing they are thinking of is, What's In It For Me?

So how can you help them?

Can you share a product / service, workshop they are teaching with your fans?

Can you help them out at an event, can you donate your time/ services or products to something they are doing?

Patronize them!

Nothing says support then actually buying someone's product or service and using it (and then give a rave testimonial).

If you want to get in front of someone, show them that you truly do care about their business and support it!

That is a surefire way to build strategic alliances with someone. They will be more willing to cross promote your business or collaborate with you on something totally fresh and new.

List 10 people that you would like to collaborate with and how you can contribute to what they are doing?

I WANT TO COLLABORATE WITH:

I CAN CONTRIBUTE TO HIM/HER BY:

I WANT TO COLLABORATE WITH:

I CAN CONTRIBUTE TO HIM/HER BY:

I WANT TO COLLABORATE WITH:

I CAN CONTRIBUTE TO HIM/HER BY:

I WANT TO COLLABORATE WITH:

I CAN CONTRIBUTE TO HIM/HER BY:

I WANT TO COLLABORATE WITH:

I CAN CONTRIBUTE TO HIM/HER BY:

I WANT TO COLLABORATE WITH:

I CAN CONTRIBUTE TO HIM/HER BY:

I WANT TO COLLABORATE WITH:

I CAN CONTRIBUTE TO HIM/HER BY:

I WANT TO COLLABORATE WITH:

I CAN CONTRIBUTE TO HIM/HER BY:

I WANT TO COLLABORATE WITH:

I CAN CONTRIBUTE TO HIM/HER BY:

I WANT TO COLLABORATE WITH:

I CAN CONTRIBUTE TO HIM/HER BY:

USING THESE STRATEGIES WILL INSTANTLY TAKE YOU FROM BASIC TO BOMBSHELL AND SPARKLE BRIGHT AND MAKE YOUR COMPETITION A NON-EXISTENT THING OF THE PAST!

Xx,

Timeesha

Made in the USA
Las Vegas, NV
21 December 2023

83404054R00059